These Hands

Poems by
James M. Keegan, S.J.

Reflection by James M. Weiss
Illustrations by Julie Gratz

ISBN: 978-1543190465

Contact Information for Author:
Campion Center
319 Concord Road
Weston, MA
(978) 828 1095 or (781) 788 4700

For editorial purposes, please contact:

Prof. James M. Weiss, james.weiss@bc.edu

CONTENTS

Acknowledgments

My thanks go to two journals who published four of my poems while I retained the copyright. In 1967 and 1968, *Poetry Northwest* published "A Gravestone Close to Home" (Vol. 9, No. 3), "Gulls in the Line of Vision" (Vol. 8, No. 1) , and "The Light Keeper" (Vol. 9, No. 3). *America* published "Falling" (July 30, 2012).

As I bring these poems to light, I am deeply grateful to my deceased parents, James and Freda Keegan, my brother Richard whose widow Linda has written award-winning poetry, and my sister Patricia who lights up every room she enters.

My early professors at Boston College taught me how to see the world and find words for what I saw. I acknowledge P. Albert Duhamel, Richard Hughes, Francis Sweeney, S.J., Leonard Casper, Edward Hirsh, and John Mahoney.

My fellow Jesuits over the years have been inspiring and faithful friends, especially Richard Bollman, Richard Roos, and William Barry.

My special gratitude goes to Joan Caldwell for her generosity with expert editorial work in formatting, layout, and publication. My lively thanks also to Julie Gratz for her evocative illustrations.

My thanks also go to Liz Ellmann who steered the ship of Spiritual Directors International and the journal *Presence*.

Among my other friends I want to acknowledge Steve Wirth and Sarah Comeau.

I also thank James Weiss, who helped make this book and to whom it is dedicated.

DEDICATED

To

James M. Weiss

SPRING

If you can tell me how the frequent burst
of pheasants from the brush, the swagger
of the moon-struck waves, the dark receding
of the snow and, in the morning sprawl,
the news of robins, all are spring,
can you explain how spring
and you arise so clearly in my mind,
together?

FACES

I

You should know that my view of the world is skewed.
For the past few years, my head has been collapsing
    into my chest.
My eyes can focus on one-third of the scene before me.
My eyes, at rest, look straight at your belt buckle.

II

I remember the Old Man of the Mountain in the forests
    of New Hampshire.
Birthed and abandoned by the glacier heading north,
    he became his own sculptor,
creating himself, rock slip after rock slide until in a
    tangle of pine root,
mud and gravel, schist and granite a Great Stone Face
    emerged, serenely poised
over the lake and valley below. Centuries of winter left
    their wounds.
The fissures brought the men with ropes and chains,
    planks, shims and cement
to hold him against another season.
Between midnight and one on May 3, 2003,
    he crumbled and fell.

Some said they heard a long sigh
    when the Old Man shuddered,
turned and took his place again
     in the eternal mountain.

III

We bought a Ford sedan in 1954,
    controlled by a joystick on the floor.
    It sported a dome roof and a "frowning chrome grill."
    It seemed sometimes to be laughing at us.

We called that car *The Feather Gray* because
    that's what it said on the brochure.
    An excellent backdrop
    for family photos, a part of the family.

Sundays my father would ask, "Who's for a little ride?"
    meaning, of course, we're all going for a ride!
    We would stop at the Old Man's car park
    to pay our respects, walk down to the lake ...

... a driver with a green car
had swiped *The Feather Gray*, scarring the passenger door
and popping from its socket the right headlight,
giving the car
the look of a Cyclops with a burning stick
in his one good eye.
The light was replaced and remounted,
the scar still showing

through cheap paint. A new maroon Pontiac Bonneville
caught its due attention while the Ford lingered
like the ancient gentleman in Bed 6, whose latest fall
emboldens friends to say he hasn't been the same since.

AUGUST, 1945

The uncles had already come home,
enlarging stories of war gone mad:
a parachute that would not open,
a snake that would not die,

the flash of a drawn knife,
the *rhumpa rhump* of heavy artillery
taking down an ancient village;
back now and safe from the dawn

that drags behind itself the muddy
remnants of the day before, the boots
of those so newly dead, the secret
wish to join them in their rest.

> Fireworks
> in those days
> were shot off
> one at a time.
> They were safer
> for all but the daring
> boys who ran
> to check the duds.
> I dreamed of them
> till Nazis rose
> from the duds
> to vaporize
> the city hall.

This morning's radio carried the news:
Seventy thousand men, women and children
died immediately when an A-bomb dropped
on Hiroshima, Japan. The war is over.
The town celebrated on the beach that night
with honking horns and speeches,
beer, whiskey, and fireworks.
Into the din my father spoke:
God help them poor Japs. God help them.

ICICLES, TALK, GOOD BEER

These elders, wriggling out for beer,
expanding of old log fires,
note the arm on the barkeep's boy
pelting snow at the icicles.

"You have to hit it square and hard,
not on the tip! But hard at the root,
and the thing comes floating down
like a damned angel."

Big ones we'd cover and pack with snow
for igloos. When it grew small
sometimes you sucked it down to the mitten.
Always my leather gloves were stained

white when the heat got to them.
-- One thinks he'll change the subject.
"Go back to when the roof fell in
square on the widow's son."

The ice that year hung off the porch
like mad teeth in the ground;
and the old lady in the hip-deep snow
beating her wrists on the ice.

"The snow on my roof is sloughing down,
curling up to the window,
ready to slide. It skews
the icicles in at angles,

puffs them up at the joints." Another
hand goes out for beer
and houses hang in the winter sun,
all their discipline downward.

A GRAVESTONE CLOSE TO HOME

Just as he used to purse his lips,
then crook and nod his head when something
hurt, my father died with perfect
acquiescence. The rest of us
came unprepared. The house began
the formal closing-up; windows
fell along the rooms;
we in the fixed air,
poised like a struck beast,
breathed to the stroke of a hallway door.

We're back to truth since that November.
With a smile remember the little games
we played beside the water, his lady
rummaging among the waves to find us
out. We can delineate our memories
and now have placed his death among them;
we notice others go and not
impair reality.

But sometimes when she hears my voice
my mother has to catch herself
from panic, and once while she was dozing
her hand went out to where he sat,
and turned to rock when she remembered.
Even I've come shouting out of dreams,
to find them true.
                All the strangers
filling the room are terribly familiar.

ASIA

The old fathers' shirts would tumble out of the dryers
                just before ours went in.
They once were white but after a thousand washings,
they emerged yellow and brown like old *New York Times*.

We laughed.

Down the front ran juice- or butter-shaped
                continents and rivers, natural borders,
great beasts circling jungles or Leviathan
                frolicking to no one's harm,
etched forever into the tumble dried cloth.
Praise for last week's ranch dressing,
                chicken stew, squash pie.

We laughed.

Between the teeth of a fading alligator hung
                a pasta sauce lamb,
no longer red but, with its many deaths
                a musty rose.
The beast and its prey were one.
We found the only still-white spot on
                an otherwise indelible
yellow t-shirt and declared it The North Pole.

We laughed. There was only Asia to discover now.

Last night at the end of dinner,
a fresh cut of salmon with peas, carrots, and rice
　　　　had tilted my balance.
I looked with disgust at the trail of pink fish
pursued by a posse of green peas
from my shirt down to the edge of the plate,
the lip of the table and down,
into areas which my crowded bib could not guard.
A friend's voice, from the left:
　　　　"You did fine work wrestling the salmon."

I laughed. We laughed.

GULLS IN THE LINE OF VISION

The gulls are breaking morning on the eastern beach;
the rocks are shaken, the air is uncontrolled
and moves in deep satin sounds, scraps
along the water bristle, lop back
in a dead ballet and the air collects a poignant
imprecision. The gulls have taken over.
Caped in their morning haw, all throat,
the grander and the younger shift from foot to foot
to provide a bass line and raucous newlyweds
arrive from other beds, compose in wide
crescendos an ellipsis pierced, exploded by the motion
of the swirl; as he turns in the high air, one
is a wobbling ring on a stick, others land
pulling down their feathers like umbrellas on the sand.
The clouds are rolling down the sun, the beach
is pink, the tide comes in with parts of crabs.

FOX

I sat at the summit of Iroquois Park, above acres of tumbled
    roots and undergrowth that fall into the back of
        Kroger's market in the valley below.

An adult fox stepped from the thicket, saw me and twitched
    in surprise. He stared for a long fox-time, debating
        whether to go or stay. He held my eye,

cocked his head quizzically, as if to ask about trust. I did not
    move or breathe but kept his eye for an eternal minute.
        His ribs showed through his coat. I wondered

what he ate, and where. With elegance untouched by poverty
    he slipped into the brushy wood. I heard his song.
        Welcome to my hill. Remember me.

Animals know sooner, possibly better than we the coming fury,
    earthquakes, a hard rain, tsunamis, tornadoes, car bombs,
        the end of the world.

Animals feel it. They howl or bray or screech, they whine or cry,
    they bellow, bawl, or tuck their tails under their backsides.
        They know how much we look, how little we see.

THE DYING GULL

You and I were questioning the tide
that beached the dying gull, revolving and revolving
in the little sand; it has no other eye
undrowned behind the clumps of sky,
wrinkled suns in the heaped green
or the dark of the one beach and the one
hole in the cold sand
where this bird now is staring.

As yesterday we, desiring, silent, flanked the dying gull,
that great unclouding eye provoked conceptions
of your death or mine
as vivid colloquies of light
flung out from a center,
a separation, neither pain nor horror,
of the eyes from time,
holding all the waters, binding the air
to a stillness.

There was evening dark in your eyes
as the sun went over your shoulder.

TWO DOGS AND SPRING

You know those dogs, the brown dishevelled mutt
who haunts the backstairs for pity and the motley
black-and-brown-patch mongrel we watched once
case a rabbit odor, descend implacable,
then sniff a silent pardon from the empty bush.
Have you remarked that when they follow –
as they always do – your walks,
they try their damnedest to be debonair, casual;
and often, twenty feet ahead of you,
one stops, feigns a condescending interest
in low-slung shrubs and just before
he nuzzles in, casts one neurotic eye
back to find out if you've turned around?
You know those two. This morning they were there
unshakable. I left them staring blandly
at the pure affront of six black mallards' necks
coiling down for fish some ten yards out,

and thought again I'd lost them. One can't count
on insults, not with these. A sudden squirrel
caught their other eye and three in line,
squirrel-dog-dog flashed across me
straight with a dog scream. The squirrel swooped
a travelling arc, an elm arc, and turned
the tree all circles and ellipses in the air.
The mallards lifted gently out of water rings,
and he who slips away, with a talent for the wild,
looped the branches up the sky and came
by quite another set of trees to earth.

BEARS WATCHING

I

This morning the police came to us with a warning
someone had spotted one –
or maybe it was two –
brown bears

in the woods around our house, and please
would we advise our guests
of the same. No

walks in the woods. Someone had overheard
the news and already the house
buzzed with adventure

and advice. Stay indoors. If you must go out,
carry a loud rattle or a stick to bang
on a trash can cover.

Or sing if you must, something loud and operatic.
"But won't that let them know
where we are?" "Yup.

If she comes too close punch her in the nose.
Don't look her in the eye. Act ashamed.
If you spy a cub walk backward fast."

According to a survey no mammal in Weston is larger
or more dangerous than the adult human male,
but – now, for one – or two – wild bears.

What will you say, Gentlemen of Weston?
Do you have a word to keep future bears
at bay? On a Sunday in November 2011
the seven billionth life on earth was born
to a mother in China or India.
"These children will come to you," prophesied
the holyman of Bihar: India, hunger-home
to empty eyes, balloon bellies. "Will you see God in them
or a devil?" Days there were punctured by tubercular
hacking. Nights belonged to the jackals, distant enough
to sound like children at play, close enough to disembowel
one's sleep. "These children will come for food.
What word will we have for them?"

III

Bears have settled into other towns:
Stockbridge, Andover, Amherst; soon another suburb.
People worry, of course. Advice stiffens into law;

small dogs and children must remain indoors,
bears may be shot on sight,
no immigrants need apply.

MOTHS

for Frank Herrmann, S.J.

No, these were not the hungry gypsy moths
that chewed their way through Connecticut
to the New York line, leaving every crotch
in every tree slimed with their progeny.

No, beauty is neither traded nor scorned
among the royalty of butterflies, the Monarch,
whose thousand miles of flights ensure blood-
lines of flaming colors, patterns, grace.

I have heard that a fluttering butterfly in Boston
can prompt a windstorm in Delhi. Wondrous feat!
The moth we saw, under creamy green sails,
put down in a tangled garden of lavender and mint;

a second, identical, and then a third formed
a spiraling cone of green wings, a window
in the air, leaving as softly as they came:
nature's revelations everywhere.

THE LIGHT KEEPER

Some phrase of all I used to sing,
to feel the morning, teeming with the sea,
buzz across my brow,
to walk the morning to the tower,
to put it out
and hear myself devoured by the rocks,
spat like a wave, devoured – some phrase
still hums in these last lightings of the lamp.
Perhaps the last inflections of the sun
are tricking on the western rocks tonight.
It is no matter. Tomorrow, should it speak,
I will intone another dance along the glaze;
should it not, I will become
the water's and the sun's smooth stone.
Business now is with the night.
The gulls are gone; the buoy-bell disembodied.
I conceive the humped black sea
torn by a mountain of crags
and night itself like a quivering woman,
amazed by the tower, the light.

AFTER LUNCH

I lay and listened as an apple I'd devoured
an hour before wailed and grappled with the walls
of my intestines, ducking juices and gassy squirts
from the rolling funhouse-tunnel floors
that run so close below my surface. The fruit,
of course, did not survive the mystery of me.
You will, though I am a carnivore, you will emerge
alive from my obscurest parts – and more –
will find a heart that knows its hunger (not
Moloch grinding in his caves for food), a heart
refreshed, younger for your passing-through.

I lay and laughed with all my innards laughing.

NOT SO MUCH THE MOON

Not so much the moon as words about the moon,
shadows you and I create on the sterile sand
or discover, floating in the tide's calligraphy
the words we offer, cupping all the oceans
for a moment in these hands – this full word, ripe,
slips to another phase, shapes itself
in the night, collides with morning and dissolves.

The word that I would consummate with you
would shatter at your feet like an alabaster jar.

This evening I can offer you but pieces,
broken light in the water dripping from my fingers,
the fragile hands of Jesus at another moon,
lifting, as if all his love were in it, broken bread
and words that rattled in the pale spring night
like bones.

SONNET

Parkinson's, like some dark angel's bleak
  embargo on my need to stand and speak,
  goes on from there to say, "You're looking well,"
  and leaves me on the tidal shores of hell.

God's sweeter angel is bested in the brawl
  with nothing comforting to say but, "Fall,
  fall into truth: there is no leaving
  here, only time and space for weaving

Your pain, your anger, your lies to yourself and others,
  into the sullied flag that waves and hovers
  over all who wait for truth to be revealed.
  It is then, not now, you will be healed."

My heart, my feet feel forward. That's the curse!
  My brain, my nerves, my life are in reverse

ON HEARING THAT I WILL NOT WALK AGAIN

OKAY. That's it. It's
over.   Full stop.

The brain has decided: enough
dopamine already wasted
on brittle muscle and sinew,
hamstring and torn tendon.

I heard Death rattle by.
I said I will go with you
if you want. The trees
by the water said, not
yet.

How can one say farewell to the ocean
which carries no such sympathy,
needs no sorrow to fill its abyss,
nothing yawning to speak?

Here, between the seasons, there is no sound
but the tired wash of glistening black water
against the darker black of beach. I know this place,
have laughed and burrowed in the sand, have held
your children here as Cape Neddick lays a solid arm
along the sea, and stills it. Tonight the place is lost
on both sides in the fog. And I am startled
by three silhouette figures on a bench before me.
One strums a guitar. All three sing quietly.

The streetlights are making halos in the mist.

FALLING

It is no matter you were carrying the heirloom platter
   and five silver forks for cheesecake later on.

It is of little concern your cigarette took the opportunity
   to sculpt and burn its brown face into your acrid rug.

On a clear morning where the dawning sun
   will slash the straight line of ocean
   you may see a green flash on the horizon, a blessing.
You may or may not see it.
So much hangs upon the quality of your attention.

So much depends upon
the multiple mind to remain faithful to the waves
of gleaming silverware, the dancing cigarette,
   faithful even to the surprise tremor
   in your lower lip at breakfast:
   the menace in the ordinary,

Too much for the brain to absorb
    absent the pleasures of dopamine.
Fear, that night crawler,
whose descent into your shoes while you sleep
whose precise leap from an overhead branch
    to your shoulder
whose starring season in the Garden story
    takes down reason
breaks down communication nerve to muscle
snakes down through your darkest treasures
    to a common vault of shame.

    O Lord, come to my assistance.
    O God, make haste to help me.

THESE HANDS

When did these hands become foreign to me?
Skewed like a lobster's claws: about ten degrees
off at the wrist – and boney? Puffy blue rivers
of blood run north-northwest up their back side.

And when did these hands make enemies of
buttonholes, zippers, clasps, snaps, fasteners of
all sorts, screws, safety pins, paper clips or
any kind of knot? Did it happen in my sleep?

My sleep has been visited in recent weeks by a
newborn boy in a crowd. He looks at me and laughs,
stretches out to me ten perfect fingers and
holds my scarred flesh in his divine grasp.

SWIMMING IN JAMAICA

Once, swimming in Jamaica,
I put the reef between me and the beach
and stopped: the sea had arched beneath me
unawares, grinning from its fullness,
a creature suddenly aroused at home,
an enemy. Not courage – more the will
to have it out with wildness – forced me
down until I kicked the bottom.
I burned my thigh along the reef,
I was alone and very much afraid.

Consider Beowulf, that "flower of warriors,"
who, like Christ, his avatar, descended for days
into the toxic lake to slay the monsters Grendel
and his Mother. The deed complete, his mentor
Hrothgar warns him that his bloom will surely fade,
his strength and skills no longer serve, and soon
"repellent age" will decay his fragile beauty.
Grendel did not die. His Mother did. Be aware.

So it is tonight, though far
more primitive – not ready now for words
or even understanding – for we have not
made peace yet, the reef, the sea, and I.

THE COLD

The moon that morning flattened out the sky
and pinned it like a map behind him.
Once more she watched him haul the logs
across blue snow and, square between
the window and the woods, fix all the fury
of his dreams on the floating axe. Then strike.
He never told his dreams; they'd not
concern her. But days he woke like this
the room went brittle, water hissed
in her burning corner. When, cold and carrying
the frozen wood, he knelt before the fire,
white distance spread like nebulae between them;
and when he sat, she came to know
the hands that crouched beside his plate like hounds
were stalking something bloody in the snow.

Inspired by The Virgin Spring, a film by Ingmar Bergman

CEMETERY AT MY WINDOW

Touch me and convince me I am here.
Sometimes I'm not as certain as I was
before disease erupted in my sphere.
Last night the automatic balefire[1] buzzed
across the street, hummed like a planet. Stiff,
remote, my body ached for earth as if
the dead were chafing in their frozen lawn.
We touch like children playing, and move on.

---

[1] Balefire refers to battery-powered vigil lights.

SONNET ON THE WORD AS FIRE

I own a voice for telephones, budget meetings,
cogent phrases hammered to a secretary's ear,
letters piled like lines of polished fittings,
hollow as a buoy bell when you appear.

Your presence, like an ocean, cancels my mind's mapping;
horizons, houses, ribs come loose, words crumble to the floor,
roll to the room's edges; another word is shaping
in the booming night; storm tides erase the shore,

the page is blank, the language loses mooring
hourly. Away from phones, beside a fire in Maine
I wait, illumined by the inarticulate roaring
logs, for some dark winter to desert my brain.

I have no words. These are already burning.
Sit with me, see their shadows turning.

THE RAIN
for David

He excommunicated the church, its
muttering mercies, wet pyres waiting in the courtyard;
dimming the way of dialogue without
engagement, prayer without humility.

The rains ran hard and constant, flooding out
the first lines of spring. Easter without
new life. *Disordered* is the word on the armband
or, more likely, the headpiece on his cross.

He found a teacher who for years held him,
whose own lake lay caked and dry, runoff
never meeting porous soil,
whose word remained: that God is found

in suffering, God's church in the pain of another.
The rock rolled back. Light poured upon
A thousand blossoms flowering in volcanic cracks
And faces of faithful who, with him, now rose.

TOURING

What can I say to her when she stops chattering?
Another day, a bus to leave Madrid
for Avila. King Philip's house of death[2]
has dropped behind a hillock to the right; the day
bends carefully around the cross of brothers[3]
for a day's peace, and passes on.
We ride a scarred plain, fast among
rock hulks dreaming like a mummy herd
of bison. I walk with shards of sunlight down
from the walled city to Teresa's Convent.

The moment's grace, the fire in the heart,
love's words, the Lord on the stairs, these pass.
Saint John must rise and afternoon comes down,
and she must go. They have no stone to hold
their words; nothing is hewn between them but the air,
now silent, where she pressed her shoulder to the grille
to hear. They loved each other and they said goodbye.

---

[2] This refers to El Escorial, the monastery-cum-palace built
by King Philip II of Spain (d. 1598) to rest his father's bones
and his own.
[3] The cross of brothers refers to the Valle de los Caidos,
Valley of the Fallen, built by Francisco Franco as a tomb for
himself and for those partisans who fought and died for him
in the Spanish Civil War of the 1930s.

ESPAÑA

Though my life convinces me the more
I live, the more I like to live – to stand
like sudden bone before the tombs of kings
or mountains, to lose myself in Greco's *El Expolio*,[4]
to fall in love again, to hear the voice that sings
like water in my own most vibrant center
and blush for a God so intimate – although I know
these moments, and they flesh my stone,
your presence, like a match struck in a theatre,
locates in me the pain of knowing them alone.

---

[4] "El Expolio" refers to El Greco's painting, "The Disrobing of Christ".
It hangs in the sacristy of the Cathedral of Toledo, Spain.

DARWIN TO HIS WIFE

Autumn's not the tree's best time.
Things come down. What cannot fall
rots. I embraced you free. But I'm
not wood. Forgive me if each letting-go
is difficult. My brain is sure: what clings
is lost, dies now or generations
later in its comfortable mud
while creatures lungèd and leggèd
cohabit on unimaginable plains.

THE UNSHOD FILING OF THE RAIN

The unshod filing of the rain along the roof
has worn apart the seams, and since I once
had troubled to look into caulking, I could do more
than line the floor with pails in this wet year.
There are, since that one wildness, thirty measured
years; until this time no day when cyclic
scarlet did not sweep across the brick,
purple leaf a ticking tree, and then
another sleep. Oh, then it was not night,
not day: fish burned in the stream, birds,
when you called, flashed, hollowed the air, and the sun
sat on a shining rock. My dear, my dear,
how did ten thousand fallings fleck that sun,
gauge our time? how end it ? we return
and catalogue the bird?
                    I do not call
these memories; that cannot be; say
they are the sudden spirits of an aging man
who, since the eave is broken, dances barefoot
to the nights eroding, jagger-voiced in pails.

THE CALM

To Sir Francis Chichester

When down the coast of Africa the wind
ran pleasant and exact, kaleidoscopic
stars came blooming, the sun flung
magnet arcs before him; while
the automatic tiller reined
the wind, he snapped by some remote-
control specific color photos
of himself at work. This all
had been arranged with astronomical precision.

                      Good Hope lay south and east
when clapping on the gunwales ceased, the jib hung straight,
the sea in its own circle simmered. He tried to wait,
inventing work or dozing in the sun. But when at night
stars stood propped like ancient crockery
      doubled in the marble sea,
a vagrant in a locked museum, awed by the stopped stone
fluid now in the moon's mosaic, huddled
      against his memory.
He'd come to tempt the wind; the wind was folded
like a silent guru into every moving thing.

A flying fish curled the air,
the tape recorder whirled dispassionately
        Beethoven's *Emperor*,
the mast revolved in a hollow orbit. In a dead spiral
        the *Gipsy Moth*
beat up the front of the sun, beat down the back.
He at the center turned,
listening
hearing the rim of the waters wash in his veins,
heard the horizon contracting, expanding,
heard in his sole center the swell, the billow and the breaking.
        Here on the silent water, firm on his hand
        the mast-pole rose, sails bellied-up;
        a double ridge of foam behind the tiller
        banked the harrowed sea in the wind's wake,
        lay in the heavy sea a new equator.

GIVE THE BODY OVER
In Memory of a Great Priest

Give the body over to the shovel.
Let it slip beneath the turf,
Fill it in with stones and rubble.
Let him rest. He's had enough.

Meek religion, easy grace,
Failed attempts to measure heaven.
He met demons face to face
Sat in jail for his convictions.

Let no easy resurrections
Ever dull his fiery pain.
He had no time for self-protection
Claiming, "I'll be back again."

Enemies and friends would ask
"Are you the one who is to come?
Or should we look to find another?"
He replied as always, "Yes."

JUNIOR McNEIL

Whatever's easiest gives less pain —
      like writing this?

I have a voice
    a standard meter
       monotone
         a bored, tired, anxious-for-nothing voice.
How can I reclaim the things I should have done
but did not do?
     Junior McNeil, left in Jamaica,
     rotting in jail, now dead I hear from John,
     found in the bushes in back of St. George's,
     disowned by his father;
         handkerchiefs lying unironed
           in my closet;
    prayer.

    NO. I CANNOT.
God, you! Collect my scraps.
     Don't coddle me, don't teach me your name.
       God!

LEVERKUSEN

In Leverkusen just outside Cologne,
behind my brother's house a railroad track
unused, completely overgrown
with mint and wild white lilac . . .

Do these rails bear the triumph
Of breaking glass, of burning books,
of neighbors somehow missing?
Are these atrocities not loud enough
To be heard by stone and steel?

If they could speak their savage truth,
would they shudder, bury themselves in earth,
melt from shame, derail the train?

Like Simon the Cyrenean unaware of what he held
They could not know the freight they bore.

I have no business here.
I will be silent, must be mute
Like God who vanished.
There are no words.
Words have died, God with them.

The tracks have vanished into overgrowth.

MAD MUSIC

That morning in the grey cathedral
radiator pipes behind the altar
had a Visitation.
A steam quartet *allegro furioso*
shook out broken patterns from a land of fire
and flaps of local gossip from a land of bones,
a rather shocking revelation:
only Someone wild could play
the grey cathedral pipes that way.
Around the marble mist we prayed
strange dances on a wrinkling kneeler.

POETIC JUSTICE

Perhaps poetic justice now
requires that an end
be made of metaphor to speak
the literal to a friend.

Perhap frustration's faculty
is wonder when the snow
doubles down the ancient trees,
dumb with what they know.

I can't pronounce the winter out
nor with a promise clear
the storms that rumble landscapes down
till outlines disappear.

Then let my burden be the woods
and you in gentle mind
wander deeper in than words
I cannot think to find.

AND GIVE OUR BEST TO UNCLE

Before my teeth fall out
and more joints start to click
like metronomes collecting silence,
I want to say, "I love you," once
and have it understood
the way the mirror
understands my face.

A Reflection on the Poems of James Keegan

Jim Keegan opens himself and his readers to large realities embedded in simple experiences. This is fitting, because that matches the original meaning of the Christian experience and mystery called incarnation. Thus, for example, as he remembers his early years in a New Hampshire town, he recaptures the childhood security of community rituals; but on mature reflection, he sees the ambiguity lurking in them and finds there premonitions of life and death. ("Faces", "August, 1945", "Icicles, Talk, Good Beer")

Similarly, for him as a coastal New Englander, the ocean is an abiding presence. He communicates awe, beauty, and sometimes terror at its vastness, its movements both regular and unexpected, and even its dreadful silence when becalmed. ("The Light Keeper", "The Dying Gull", "Swimming in Jamaica", "The Calm") He watches for the wisdom in animals' movements, comical and ominous by turns. ("Fox", "Bears Watching", "Moths" "Two Dogs and Spring") He revels in the color, motion, harmony, and cacophony of nature, all of which enliven his senses and heighten his perception. ("Gulls in the Line of Vision", "Two Dogs and Spring", and others)

He also presents intimate engagements with friendship and human love, sometimes lyrically ("Poetic Justice", "And Give Our Best to Uncle"), sometimes in more ambiguous tones. Natural occurrences can summon up identification with a loved one. ("Spring", "After Lunch") Conversely, a friend's presence enables him to plumb a difficult experience on the shore. ("The Dying Gull") A friend's absence imparts joy to one experience ("Spring"), pain to another ("España"). He is sharply aware that friendship and love involve both intimacy and letting go of the beloved, which he views in varying moods, now as a serene and holy detachment ("Touring"), now as a hard natural inevitability ("Darwin to His Wife"). Sometimes, his poems reach beyond identifiable states of feeling to capture an intimacy that exceeds one's power to name. ("Not the Moon", "Sonnet on the Word as Fire")

Keegan shares with his reader another intimacy, his relationship to the Parkinson's disease with which he has lived for over a decade. One cluster of poems covers a spectrum from humor to irony to poignancy to grief to rage. As his Parkinson's entails the loss of manual dexterity ("These Hands"), it evokes in one and the same poem ("Asia") both the rollicking memories of early adulthood when, as a young Jesuit, he laundered the shirts of elderly priests, and at the same time a laughing acceptance of his present disability and his own soiled shirts. As he continues to face the disease, he plumbs wellsprings of shame ("Falling") and helpless fear ("Sonnet"), sometimes breaking through to serenity ("On Hearing") and even interior healing ("These Hands").

Occasionally, these poems allude to another relationship, the relationship to God. Keegan's whimsical humor comes out in a poem ("Mad Music") contrasting God's comical spontaneity with the dry rigors of methodical prayer once practiced as a young novice. Another poem ("Junior McNeil") conveys the discovery that God may withdraw from one's attempts to pray because a more urgent reality demands one's full attention. The intimacy of a bond with God peeks through three lines (ll. 5-7) of "España". Its healing power emerges in "These Hands". His poems remind us, however, that divine love transcends both religious platitudes ("Give the Body Over") and the sins of the Church ("The Rain – for David"). He calls attention to the elusiveness of God and the hard truths of a faith rooted in the Cross ("The Dying Gull", "Leverkusen", "Junior McNeil"). This gives him courage to face raw realities without resort to "easy resurrections . . . easy grace, failed attempts to measure heaven". ("Give the Body Over")

Indeed, and perhaps surprisingly, the relationship to God feels more explicit in Keegan's poems as God recedes from view, much like unnamed friends in other poems of his who become more sharply felt as they are missed or longed for. Thus, "God's sweeter angel is bested in the brawl" with Parkinson's which is "like some dark angel" ("Sonnet"). But God goes stunningly silent, absent, even dead in the face of monstrous injustice, whether in the murder of an obscure ex-con whom Keegan knew in Jamaica ("Junior McNeil") or Hitler's unspeakable Holocaust ("Leverkusen"). Human suffering blocks the vision of God, a recurrent theme in modern religious thought. One poem ("The Cold") does not mention God at all as it describes a marriage gone very bad. Nevertheless, one beholds in that poem a likeness to the lowest circle of hell that Dante found to be not fiery but frozen because no love can warm it. The frigid Scandinavian winter mirrors the cold from lack of all communication, the frozenness still oddly preferable to a brutal fury threatening to break forth from it.

The reality of death pervades these poems, although not in a morbid or obsessive or fatalistic way. Early memories include the awareness of the tragic or premature death of others. ("August 1945", "Icicles, Talk, Good Beer", "A Gravestone Close to Home") Later experience presents him with the death confronting our whole environment ("Fox", "Bears Watching"). Indeed, nature speaks to Keegan of death as often as it does of beauty or harmony or serendipity. The awareness of death is simply part of paying attention to reality. In this regard, it should be noted that the practices of contemplative prayer as well as of the spiritual direction which Jim Keegan has offered and taught professionally are both sometimes defined as "a long, loving look at the real". Thus, death can inspire foreboding ("Fox"), or a strange serenity ('The Dying Gull'), or even humorous good cheer ("And Give Our Best to Uncle"). When I asked him about this, he offered a metaphor that deserves to be pondered. "Death," he said, "is like an underground fire that gives warmth to things on the earth and makes us want to see them and appreciate them."

Overall, God may seem a less frequent presence in Keegan's poems unless one recalls the core disposition of Jesuit spirituality in which he is steeped, namely, to find God in all things – even suffering, even death, perhaps especially in suffering and death.

One entire week of the four-week *Spiritual Exercises* of St. Ignatius, a foundational experience for every Jesuit, consists of meditation on the suffering and death of Jesus. This insight to "God in all things" enables us to revisit Jim Keegan's poems and contemplate "that which is of God", to us a Quaker phrase, in the ocean, the shore, the animals, the birds, the landscape, and the love of friends. In a personal conversation, Keegan once spoke of his poems in terms of "incarnational concreteness", meaning the sacred presence, or presences, embedded in daily reality, waiting to be discovered there. This reflects a God who is humble enough to remain anonymous. To quote Hopkins,

"These things, these things were here and but the beholder
　　　Wanting . . . "
("Hurrahing in Harvest", ll. 11-12)

This concreteness of the Divine Presence may explain what Keegan called on another occasion his "concealed religiosity".

He is, after all, a "priest-poet" in that tradition of ordained Catholics and Anglicans whose calling drew them to several themes also encountered in Keegan's work. Among Catholics, three stand out, Robert Southwell (d. 1595), Richard Crashaw (d. 1649) and Gerard Manley Hopkins (d. 1889), the first and third of them Jesuits like Keegan. Among the Anglicans, one recalls John Donne (d. 1631), George Herbert (d. 1633), Thomas Traherne (d. 1674), and in our own time, R. S. Thomas (d. 2000). This is not to suggest some necessary similarity among poets who happen to be clergy, although they do often reflect on themes found here, such as the natural world, the limitations and joys of human love, and the elusiveness and joys of divine love.

As we attune ourselves to Keegan's voice, it may be of interest to note those voices which have spoken to him. He acknowledges a debt to the priest poets Donne and Hopkins. Not surprisingly for one whose poems meditate on immediate geographical locations, he names three New Englanders: Robert Frost, Donald Hall, and Mary Oliver. Among other contemporaries he cites John Berryman, Jane Kenyon, and Billy Collins. And from his earliest reading, he feels the presences of e. e. cummings, T. S. Eliot, and W. B. Yeats.

An introduction is not the place for critical analysis of poetic form, other than perhaps to note that Keegan is as much at home with stricter forms like sonnets and rhyming quatrains as he is with free verse and blank verse. As he worked or re-worked each of his poems in my presence, he impressed me continually with his strong sense of the rhythm in each line, knowing when a line must stop or break or flow on, or when a syllable count would ruin the rhythm. Sometimes we waited days or weeks for the right word, the right phrase, to find its place in a poem.

For over a year, it has been my delight to help Jim Keegan revisit and re-think each of his poems. For a few that he had left in fragmentary form, he rekindled the original inspiration and completed them. I had the gift of watching him labor week after week to name what one experience was trying to tell him. He also caught furtive phrases and images which had long begged to be excised or revised. Again and again, he drew upon those strengths that Wendell Berry calls for in a poet:

"You must depend upon
affection, reading, knowledge,
skill – more of each
than you have – inspiration,
work, growing older, patience . . ."

I do hope, however, that Jim Keegan will not follow Berry's very next bit of advice:

" . . . Any readers
who like your poems,
doubt their judgment."[1]

During our work together, by coincidence, Helen Vendler, a doyenne among contemporary poetry critics, captured in her essay on poets who revise their own work much of what transpired in Keegan's creative process last year.[2] In speaking of Emily Dickinson, she named what Keegan, like many poets, experienced in the labor of revision: "[I]t is only when the poet . . . reenters her vision, admitting to herself that it is not a word she lacks, but an as yet unexplored territory of inspiration . . . that the right word arrives to complete the poem." With generosity and transparency, Keegan let me revisit with him territories of fulfillments and disappointments, the wisdom fought for and won

---

[1] Wendell Berry, "How To Be a Poet", accessed on March 15, 2017, at https://www.poetryfoundation.org/poetrymagazine/poems/detail/41087

[2] Helen Vendler, "The Poet Remakes the Poem", *New York Review of Books*, March 10, 2016, pp. 40-42, http://www.nybooks.com/articles/2016/03/10/poet-remakes-poem/ , accessed October 23, 2016.

not only in his poems but in his practice and teaching and international leadership in the field of spiritual direction.

For the gift of letting me accompany him, and for the friendship we deepened thereby, I thank him. Together "I laughed. We laughed." ("Asia") As a poet, as a priest, as a patient, Jim Keegan lives with tough resilience, gentle compassion, wise insight into the souls of those who seek his guidance and God's, and an awareness of tragedy alongside his whimsical and unpredictable gift for comedy. As he hopes in "The Unshod Filing of the Rain", so I hope too that he may go on "danc[ing] barefoot".

James Michael Egan Weiss
Boston College

James M. Keegan, S.J.

James M. Keegan grew up in a small town in New Hampshire and majored in English literature at Boston College. He entered the Jesuits in 1962. After his ordination as a priest and a period of teaching at Fairfield College Preparatory School, he became Associate Novice Director for the New England Province of Jesuits. He then joined the staff of the Center for Religious Development, in Cambridge, Massachusetts, where he trained and supervised men and women in the practice of spiritual direction. After that, he worked for 11 years for the Archdiocese of Louisville, Kentucky, in similar training programs, and later directed the Eastern Point Retreat House in Gloucester, Massachusetts. He has served on the boards of Spiritual Directors International and Retreats International. He now serves on the editorial panel of *Presence: An International Journal of Spiritual Direction*. He has given workshops and training in spiritual direction in Norway, Jamaica, Korea, Singapore, and many sites in the United States and Canada. He has written poetry on and off for 50 years. He lives at Campion Center in Weston, Massachusetts.

James M. Keegan, S.J.